Fats Domino belts out "Blueberry Hill"
© Corbis-Bettmann, New York

Abbeville Publishing Group
22 Cortlandt Street · New York, NY 10007

England's Queen Mother waves to thousands on
her ninetieth birthday, August 4, 1990
© Corbis-Bettmann, New York

Abbeville Publishing Group
22 Cortlandt Street · New York, NY 10007

Beatles fans at Convention Hall in Atlantic City, 1964
© Corbis-Bettmann, New York

Abbeville Publishing Group
22 Cortlandt Street · New York, NY 10007

Rita Hayworth and Ali Kahn cut their wedding
cake, Cannes, France, May 28, 1949
© Corbis-Bettmann/UPI, New York

Abbeville Publishing Group
22 Cortlandt Street · New York, NY 10007

Actress Mae Murray in **Circe the Enchantress**, 1924
© Corbis-Bettmann, New York

Abbeville Publishing Group
22 Cortlandt Street · New York, NY 10007

Joe DiMaggio and Marilyn Monroe, recently divorced, attend a movie preview, June 1, 1955
© Corbis-Bettmann, New York

Abbeville Publishing Group
22 Cortlandt Street · New York, NY 10007

President Richard Nixon at his inaugural ball,
Washington, D.C., January 20, 1969
© Corbis-Bettmann, New York

Abbeville Publishing Group
22 Cortlandt Street · New York, NY 10007

Acrobats atop the Empire State Building, 1934
© Corbis-Bettmann, New York

Abbeville Publishing Group
22 Cortlandt Street · New York, NY 10007

New heavyweight champion of the world, Ingemar Johansson of
Sweden, consoles former champ Floyd Patterson, June 26, 1959
© Corbis-Bettmann, New York

Abbeville Publishing Group
22 Cortlandt Street · New York, NY 10007

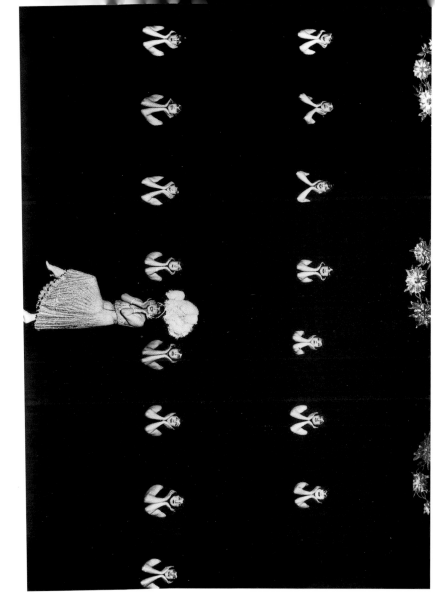

The French comedienne Mistinguette, performing
with the Folies Bergère, Paris, 1918
© Corbis-Bettmann, New York

Abbeville Publishing Group
22 Cortlandt Street · New York, NY 10007

Alfred Hitchcock and Grace Kelly on
the set of **To Catch a Thief,** 1955
© Corbis-Bettmann, New York

Abbeville Publishing Group
22 Cortlandt Street · New York, NY 10007

German director Ernst Lubitsch in **Der Blusenkönig**, 1917
© Corbis-Bettmann, New York

Abbeville Publishing Group
22 Cortlandt Street · New York, NY 10007

Modeling a hat and robe, 1909
© Corbis-Bettmann, New York

Abbeville Publishing Group
22 Cortlandt Street · New York, NY 10007

© Chronik Verlag im Bertelsmann Lexikon Verlag GmbH 1999. Printed in Hong Kong.

A newly glamorous Audrey Hepburn returns
home from Paris in **Sabrina**, 1954
© Cinetext, Frankfurt

Abbeville Publishing Group
22 Cortlandt Street · New York, NY 10007

Dustin Hoffmann plays Willy Loman and John Malkovich his son, Biff, in a television film of Arthur Miller's **Death of a Salesman**, 1985
© Corbis-Bettmann, New York

Abbeville Publishing Group
22 Cortlandt Street · New York, NY 10007

Clearing gargoyles high up on the Chrysler Building, New York
© Corbis-Bettmann, New York

Abbeville Publishing Group
22 Cortlandt Street · New York, NY 10007

Frank Sinatra and Bing Crosby croon a tune
© Corbis-Bettmann, New York

Abbeville Publishing Group
22 Cortlandt Street · New York, NY 10007

Rita Hayworth on horseback, 1949
© Corbis-Bettmann, New York

Abbeville Publishing Group
22 Cortlandt Street · New York, NY 10007

Marlene Dietrich in **Morocco**, her first Hollywood film, 1930
© Corbis-Bettmann, New York

Abbeville Publishing Group
22 Cortlandt Street · New York, NY 10007

George Bush and Mikhail Gorbachev get set to sign
START I, the arms reduction treaty, July 31, 1991
© Corbis-Bettmann/Reuters, New York

Abbeville Publishing Group
22 Cortlandt Street · New York, NY 10007

Dr. Martin Luther King, Jr., kissed by his wife, Coretta, as he leaves Harlem Hospital on October 3, 1958, weeks after being stabbed in the chest at a book signing

© Corbis-Bettmann, New York

Abbeville Publishing Group
22 Cortlandt Street · New York, NY 10007

American singer Nat King Cole

Abbeville Publishing Group
22 Cortlandt Street · New York, NY 10007

Jimmy Stewart and Grace Kelly in **Rear Window**, 1954
© Corbis-Bettmann, New York

Abbeville Publishing Group
22 Cortlandt Street · New York, NY 10007

Tom Cruise and Dustin Hoffman with Hoffman's
Oscar for the film **Rain Man**, 1989
© Sipa Press, Pari/Suu-Joffet

Abbeville Publishing Group
22 Cortlandt Street · New York, NY 10007

Opera singer Maria Callas with her husband,
Italian industrialist Battista Menechini, 1956
© Corbis-Bettmann, New York

Abbeville Publishing Group
22 Cortlandt Street · New York, NY 10007

Alfred Hitchcock directs a difficult actor
© Corbis-Bettmann/Springer, New York

Abbeville Publishing Group
22 Cortlandt Street · New York, NY 10007

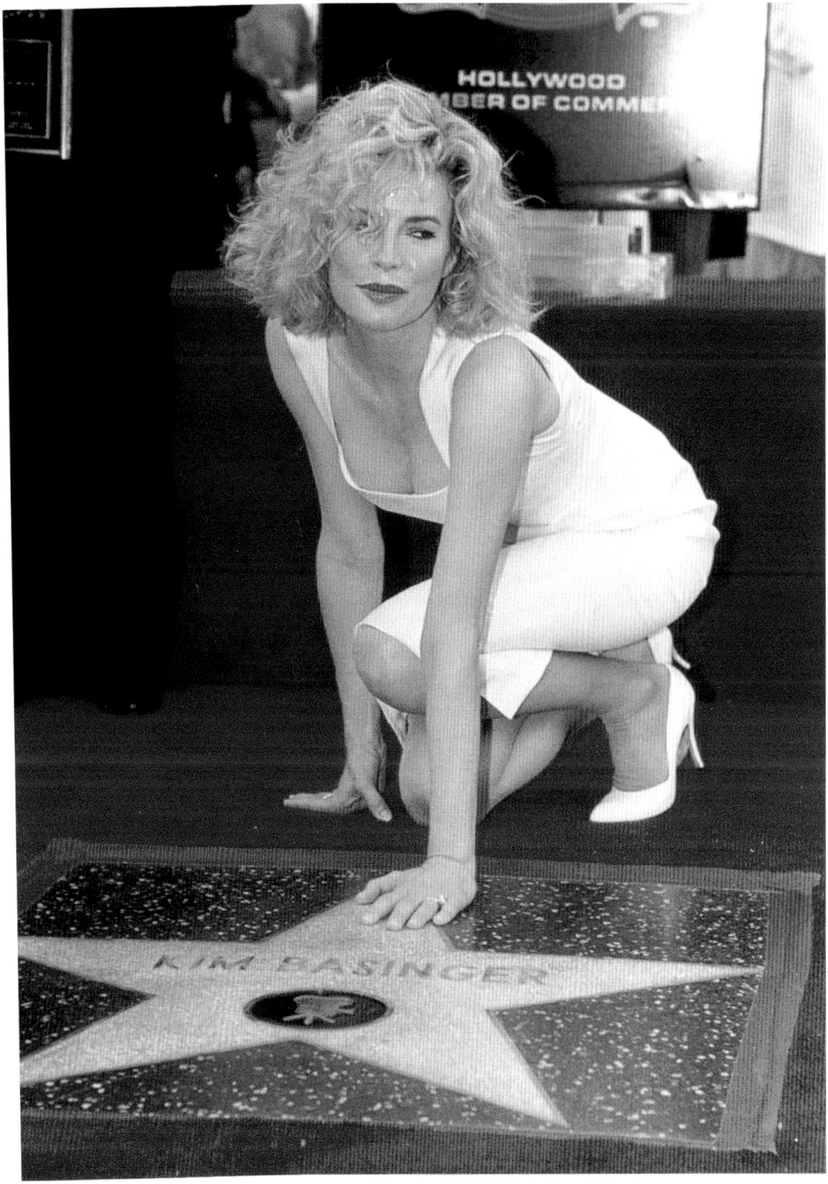
HOLLYWOOD
KIM BASINGER

American actress Kim Basinger, 1992
© Corbis-Bettmann, New York/AFP/Mike Nelson

Abbeville Publishing Group
22 Cortlandt Street · New York, NY 10007

Serving ice cream, 1910
© Corbis-Bettmann, New York

Abbeville Publishing Group
22 Cortlandt Street · New York, NY 10007